The Atl

by Bob Itali

MG (4-8)
ATOS 5.3
0.5 pts
Non-Fiction

27896 EN

Inside the NFL

THE
ATLANTA
FALCONS

TIFTAREA ACADEMY

BOB ITALIA
ABDO & Daughters

Published by Abdo & Daughters, 4940 Viking Drive, Suite 622, Edina, Minnesota 55435.

Copyright © 1996 by Abdo Consulting Group, Inc., Pentagon Tower, P.O. Box 36036, Minneapolis, Minnesota 55435 USA. International copyrights reserved in all countries. No part of this book may be reproduced in any form without written permission from the publisher.

Printed in the United States.

Cover Photo credits: Wide World Photos/Allsport
Interior Photo credits: Bettmann Photos, page 7
                Wide World Photos, pages 4, 5, 8-10, 12, 13, 15-17, 20, 21, 23, 27, 29

Edited by Kal Gronvall

Library of Congress Cataloging-in-Publication Data

Italia, Bob, 1955-
The Atlanta Falcons/Bob Italia.
  p. cm. -- (Inside the NFL)
Includes index.
Summary: Covers the history and key players of the oldest southern-based team in the National Football League.
ISBN: 1-56239-552-1
1. Atlanta Falcons (Football team)--Juvenile literature.
[1. Atlanta Falcons (Football team) 2. Football--History.]
I. Title. II. Series: Italia, Bob, 1955- Inside the NFL.
GV956.A85I83 1996
796.332'64'09758231--dc20
                                                    95-36980
                                                        CIP
                                                         AC

CONTENTS

Struggling to Soar 4
A Star-Studded Franchise 6
Norm Van Brocklin 8
Bartkowski 9
William Andrews 12
Chris Miller 16
Prime Time 20
Jerry Glanville 23
Battling Baseball 24
Jeff George 25
Glossary 29
Index 31

Struggling to Soar

In 1966, the Atlanta Falcons began playing in the National Football League (NFL). Professional football fans in Atlanta were so excited about their new franchise, the team sold 45,000 season tickets months before its first-ever game.

When the Falcons finally played that first game, they struggled. Atlanta has struggled ever since. In their relatively short history, the Falcons have won only one division title. Even more disheartening, they have made the playoffs only four times, winning only twice.

Still, Atlanta fans had hoped the Falcons would make it to the Super Bowl in 1981, the year after they won their division title. Those hopes never came true. But optimism returned in the early 1990s when Deion Sanders joined the team.

Sanders was the impact player the Falcons needed. He could break a game wide open with a dazzling interception return for a touchdown. But the Falcons never had a defense that could stop the run. To avoid Sanders, teams just ran around him.

Jerry Glanville coach of the Falcons in 1990.

Strong-armed quarterback Jeff George has taken Sanders' place in the spotlight. But it's a place where George is not comfortable, and time will tell if he can lead the Falcons to the Super Bowl.

Andre Rison reaches for a touchdown pass.

A Star-Studded Franchise

Though the Falcons have not had much team success, Atlanta has always had some of the National Football League's (NFL's) best players. Atlanta's very first draft pick was Tommy Nobis, a hard-nosed linebacker from the University of Texas.

The Houston Oilers and Dallas Cowboys wanted Nobis. But Atlanta drafted and signed him before these two Texas teams had the chance.

Nobis quickly became the heart and soul of the Falcons defense. In his first 12 games, Nobis had 150 tackles and 103 assists. He was involved in 21 defensive plays per game!

In 1966, the Falcons won three of their last five games and avoided last place. The future suddenly looked bright. The Falcons had many young and talented players. Besides Nobis, there was quarterback Randy Johnson, running back Junior Coffey, wide receiver Alex Hawkins, and defensive backs Bob Riggle, Nick Rassas, and Ken Reaves.

In 1967, Nobis, Johnson, and Coffey continued their strong play. But the Falcons had more holes in their roster than previously thought, and they finished 1-12-1. It was going to take much more time to get the quality players the Falcons needed.

Opposite page: Linebacker Tommy Nobis (60) intercepts a Johnny Unitas pass that was intended for John Mackey (88).

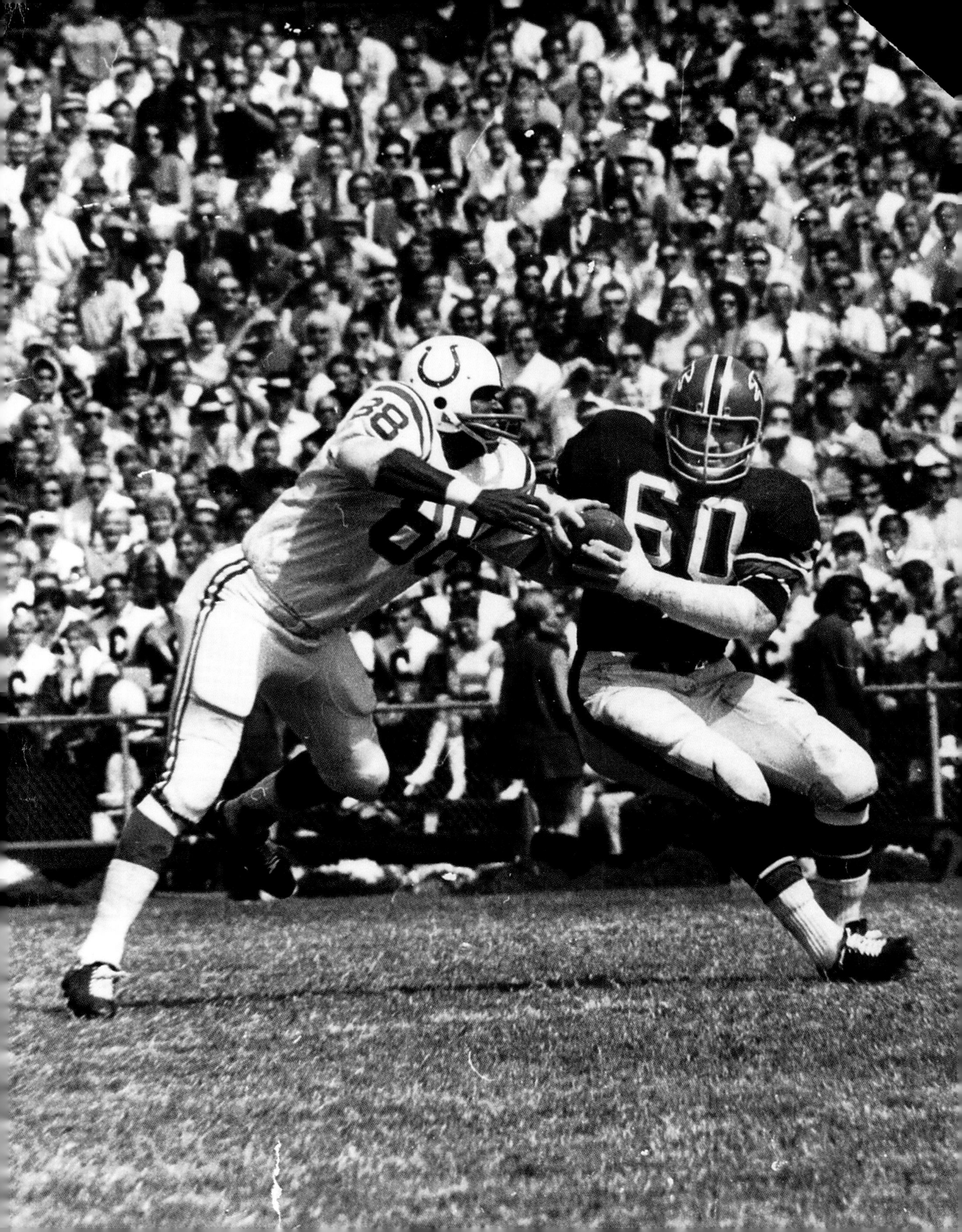

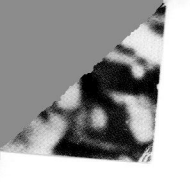

Norm Van Brocklin

In 1968, the Falcons lost their first three games. Norb Hecker was fired, and former Vikings head coach Norm Van Brocklin replaced him. Van Brocklin immediately rebuilt the team.

The new defensive star was end Claude Humphrey from Tennessee State. Humphrey and Nobis became the core of Atlanta's defense. Humphrey was named NFL Rookie of the Year. In 1969, the Falcons notched a franchise-record six victories—including a win over the Minnesota Vikings.

Coach Norm Van Brocklin was a former quarterback.

In the early 1970s, the Falcons continued to get better under Van Brocklin. In 1973, Atlanta challenged for first place with a 9-3 record. But the Falcons needed two wins to make the playoffs. Instead, they lost to Buffalo and St. Louis. It was the closest Van Brocklin would get to postseason play.

In 1974, the Falcons had high hopes. But instead, the club went backwards in the standings. Quarterbacks Bob Lee, Pat Sullivan, and Kim McQuilken could not generate much offense. And the team did not play well under Van Brocklin's stern rule.

8

Bartkowski

To make the playoffs, Atlanta needed a great quarterback. To get that much-needed player, the Falcons traded many players to Baltimore for the first-round pick in the college draft. They chose rifle-armed Steve Bartkowski from the University of California.

Bartkowski set many school passing records as he led his team to its best record in more than ten years. As a senior, Bartkowski was an All-American. Atlanta hoped he could lead the Falcons to the Super Bowl.

At first, Bartkowski made a lot of mistakes. In his first two seasons, the Falcons finished with a 4-10 record. The Super Bowl would have to wait.

Falcon quarterback Steve Bartkowski throws a pass against the Lions.

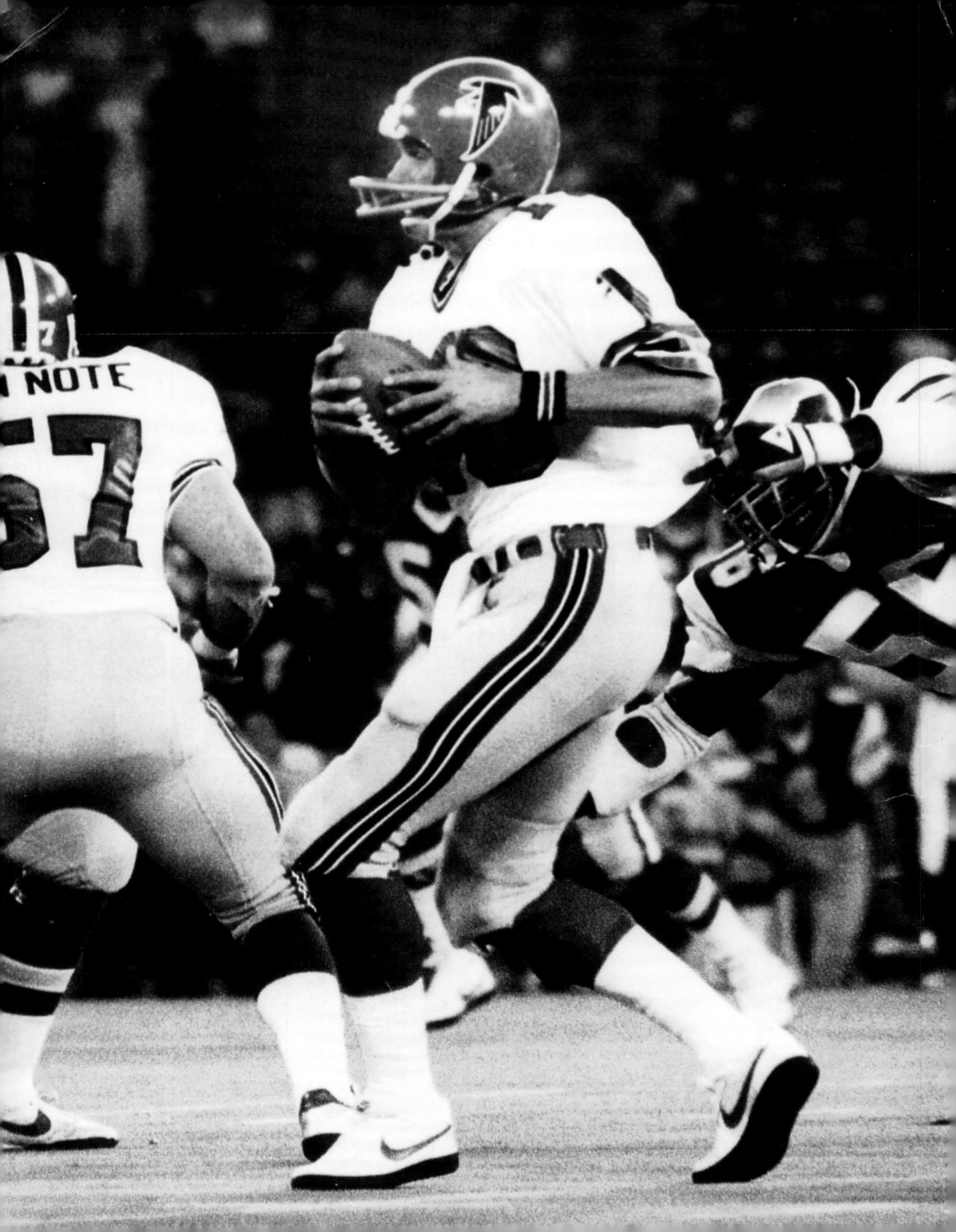
NOTE
57

In 1977, 39-year-old Leeman Bennett became head coach. Though Bartkowski missed most of the 1977 season with an injury, the Falcons finished 7-7. Even more, the defense had a record-breaking season. The Falcons allowed 129 points—the lowest ever for a 14-game schedule. Playoff hopes began to spring once again.

Bartkowski returned in 1978. But he did not play well in the preseason, and Bennett benched his young quarterback in favor of June Jones.

But after three games, Bartkowski was the starter once again. He led his team to a string of last-minute victories as the Falcons finished with a 9-7 record. For the first time in team history, Atlanta was in the playoffs.

In the first round, the Falcons faced the Philadelphia Eagles in Atlanta. The Falcons trailed 6-0 at halftime, then fell behind 13-0 in the third quarter. But the defense stiffened, and Bartkowski put together two fourth-quarter touchdown drives. The Falcons won 14-13.

The following week in Dallas, the Falcons played tough against the Cowboys. Dallas grabbed a 10-7 first-quarter lead, but Atlanta took a 20-13 lead into halftime.

In the third quarter, the Cowboys tied the game on a Danny White touchdown pass. They scored again in the fourth quarter and hung on for a 27-20 win. It was a disappointing defeat. Although Atlanta had failed to reach the Super Bowl, the Falcons expected greater things in 1979.

Opposite page: Quarterback Steve Bartkowski avoids a flying tackle in a Monday Night game, 1981.

William Andrews

But in 1979, the Falcons did not have a winning season. The only bright spot was hard-nosed running back William Andrews, who came to Atlanta from Auburn University.

At Auburn, Andrews spent most of his time blocking for teammate Joe Cribbs, who was eventually drafted by the Buffalo Bills. The Falcons wanted Andrews to block for teammate Lynn Cain. But Andrews impressed Bennett in preseason practice with his running ability. Bennett quickly realized he had more than just a good blocker. He had a great runner.

In his first two regular-season games, Andrews averaged more than 100 yards. By season's end, Andrews had set a new team rushing record with 1,023 yards.

Running back William Andrews.

In 1980, Andrews got better. He rushed for more than 1,300 yards and tacked on another 736 yards receiving—becoming one of the few running backs in NFL history to gain more than 2,000 combined rushing and pass-receiving yards.

Even better for the Falcons, Bartkowski had his best year as a professional. The Falcons finished with an NFC-best 12-4 record and won the Western Division for the first time in franchise history. Not only did their fans expect playoff success, they wanted their team in the Super Bowl.

In the first round of the playoffs, the Falcons played the Dallas Cowboys in Atlanta. The Falcons seized a 27-17 lead halfway into the fourth quarter. Atlanta was only minutes away from advancing to the conference championship.

Falcons running back William Andrews (31) runs between Redskins defenders, 1983.

But the Cowboys rallied. Dallas quarterback Danny White threw a touchdown pass to Drew Pearson that gave the Cowboys a 30-27 win. Atlanta's Super Bowl run had ended.

The Falcons had trouble regrouping in the following years. They had losing records in 1981 and 1982. Still, Andrews continued his outstanding play, as he was named to the Pro Bowl four straight times.

But in 1984, disaster struck. During preseason practice, Andrews took a handoff from Bartkowski and started up the middle. He was tackled from behind and heard something in his knee snap. Andrews was carried off the field with a serious knee injury. He would miss two full seasons.

Gerald Riggs took Andrews' place in the backfield and ran for 202 yards on opening day. But then wide receiver Billy "White Shoes" Johnson injured his knee, and Atlanta started a nine-game slide. In November, Bartkowski joined the growing list of injured players with his own knee injury. The Falcons' season was through.

In 1985, Atlanta signed first-round draft pick Bill Fralic, whom many considered a guaranteed All-Pro offensive lineman. David Archer took over at quarterback, but was ineffective. The only bright spot was Gerald Riggs, who led the NFC in rushing with 1,719 yards.

Andrews finally returned in 1986 to a hero's welcome. But it soon became clear to everyone—including Andrews—that he wasn't the powerful runner he used to be. Soon after his comeback, Andrews retired as Atlanta's all-time leading rusher.

Chris Miller

In 1987, Atlanta drafted quarterback Chris Miller, but he wasn't signed until the end of October. He played inconsistently, but showed enough promise to give the Falcons hope for the future.

Miller showed improvement in 1988 as well. So did his teammates. Second-year running back John Settle had a 1,000-yard season, and defensive back Scott Case led the league in interceptions.

But in 1989, the Falcons stumbled to a 3-8 start. Marion Campbell resigned, and new coach Jim Hanifan could not improve Atlanta's record. Stepping into the spotlight, however, was a rookie defensive back named Deion Sanders.

Quarterback Chris Miller congratulates wide receiver Michael Haynes (81) after they connected on a 75-yard touchdown pass.

Falcons quarterback Chris Miller kicks a 45-yard field goal after kicker Paul McFadden was injured.

ATLANTA FALCONS

ATL
FAL

Norm Van Brocklin joins the Falcons in 1968.

Linebacker Tommy Nobis is Atlanta's first-ever draft pick in 1966.

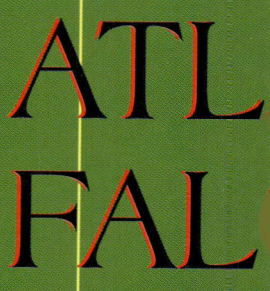

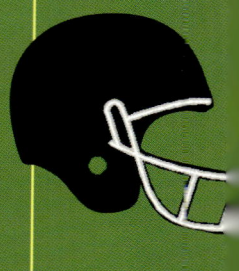

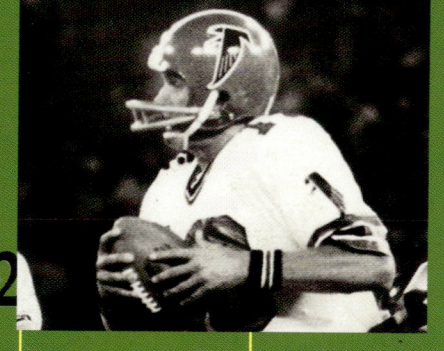

Steve Bartkowski signs with Atlanta in 1975.

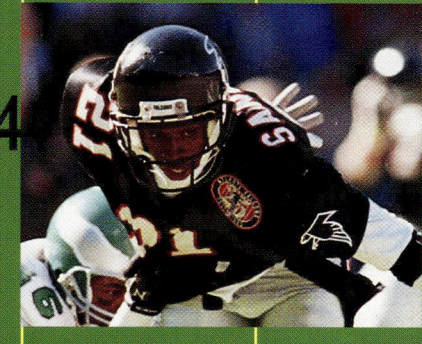

Deion Sanders is drafted by the Falcons in 1989.

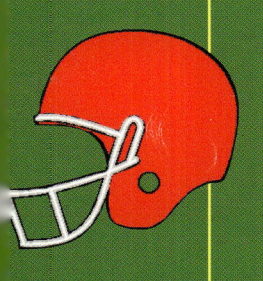

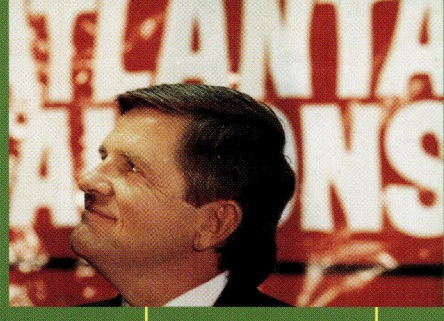

Coach Jerry Glanville joins the Falcons in 1990.

Andre Rison plays wide receiver for the Falcons in the early 1990s.

ATLANTA FALCONS

Prime Time

Deion Sanders was a talented defensive back and punt returner from Florida State. He could break a game wide open with one big play.

Sanders was a flashy player who, off the field, liked to wear a lot of gold jewelry. Because of his flashiness and his flair for dramatic, game-breaking plays, he was given the nickname "Prime Time."

Falcons Deion Sanders (21) returns a punt against the Eagles in 1990.

Deion Sanders sails for extra yardage on a punt return against the Chicago Bears in 1992.

    The Falcons had difficulty signing Sanders. He wanted a lot of money. If he did not get it, Sanders threatened to enter the college baseball draft. While in college, Sanders spent his summers playing baseball in the New York Yankees minor league organization. The Yankees had high hopes for Sanders. They were willing to offer him a lot of money to play baseball.

While Sanders' agent negotiated a contract with the Falcons, Sanders played with the Yankees. While in Seattle playing against the Mariners, Sanders got a phone call in the dugout. It was Sanders' agent. The Falcons had offered a multimillion-dollar contract. Sanders would finally join the Atlanta Falcons.

It didn't take long for Sanders to impress his new team. He worked hard and he hit even harder. In his first regular-season game, Sanders came up with a big play against the Los Angeles Rams. He caught a punt, then dropped it. As the Rams swarmed around him, Sanders picked up the ball, rolled to his right—and rambled 70 yards for a touchdown.

Sanders and Miller gave Atlanta fans some hope about their team's future. But the Falcons still had a losing record in 1989. Management felt they needed a new coach with a winning tradition. In 1990, they hired Jerry Glanville, who made the Houston Oilers into a winning team.

Falcons coach Jerry Glanville works with his defensive linemen.

Jerry Glanville

Glanville had talent with which to work. Besides Sanders and Miller, there was offensive tackle Bill Fralic and running back John Settle.

As they entered their 25th season in 1990, the Falcons finally believed they had what they needed to be a championship team. The Falcons improved their record by two wins. But it was hardly the improvement the Falcons had hoped for. A seven-game losing streak in the middle of the season destroyed any hopes of reaching the playoffs. Miller was lost in the 12th game with a broken collarbone. The Falcons' MVP that year was wide receiver Andre Rison. He set team records with 82 catches, 1,208 yards, and 10 touchdowns.

In 1991, the Falcons backed up their boasting with a 10-6 record. Atlanta ranked fifth in the NFL in points scored thanks to Miller's 26 touchdown passes. Wide receiver Michael Haynes caught only 50 passes but averaged a league-high 22.4 yards per reception and scored 12 times. Rison added 11 touchdowns. But the defense was still a problem. Sanders could defend the pass, but the defense could not stop the run.

Still, the Falcons made the playoffs. In their first round game against the Saints in New Orleans, Atlanta fell behind 13-10 at halftime. In the fourth quarter, they trailed 20-17. But a Johnson 44-yard field goal tied the score and a 61-yard bomb from Miller to Haynes iced the game for the Falcons. Now it was on to Washington to face the Redskins.

Atlanta did not have much luck in the nation's capital. Washington went up 14-7 at the half and never looked back. The 24-7 defeat was hard to take. Atlanta felt they had a better team.

Battling Baseball

The Falcons had the chance to prove they were getting better in 1992. Instead, they got worse. Sanders was too busy playing baseball and football in the fall, and the defense suffered. They ranked last in the conference. Miller was knocked out in the eighth game and lost for the season. Wade Wilson played well in his absence, but his efforts weren't enough to get the Falcons into the playoffs as they finished with a 6-10 record.

The following year, Sanders missed the Falcons first five games while playing baseball. Atlanta lost all five games. Then, with Sanders playing both defense and offense, Atlanta won six of its next eight games. Sanders led the NFC with seven interceptions. But the defense allowed a league-worst 385 points.

On offense, new quarterback Bobby Hebert passed for 2,978 yards and 24 touchdowns. Three receivers had 70 or more receptions. Rison finished with 86 catches and 15 touchdowns. Mike Pritchard had 74 catches. And Michael Haynes had 72. Erric Pegram replaced Eric Dickerson and rushed for 1,185 yards. Placekicker Norm Johnson set an NFL record with 26 field goals in 27 attempts.

But the defense was the team's downfall as it finished with a 6-10 record. Glanville was fired after the season and replaced by offensive coordinator June Jones. Even worse, Sanders placed himself on the auction block—and San Francisco came up the winner.

Jeff George

No one knew what to expect in 1994. The talented young quarterback Jeff George joined the team and promised to light up the scoreboard with his rifle arm. The Falcons lost their opener to Detroit in overtime. The following week, Rison guaranteed a win over the Los Angeles Rams. He and his teammates came through with a 31-13 win, earning June Jones his first NFL victory. Rison caught a pair of 16-yard touchdown passes, and was on an NFL-record pace with 26 receptions in two weeks.

A Week 3 loss to the Kansas City Chiefs and Joe Montana put the Falcons record at 1-2. But the following week, Atlanta rebounded with a 27-20 win over the Washington Redskins. The Falcons then earned a surprising 8-5 win against the Los Angeles Rams with their defense, which tacked on a 2-point safety. At 3-2, the Falcons found themselves in first place in the NFC West.

In Week 6, cornerback Vinnie Clark set up 10 points with a pair of interceptions. Jeff George threw 36- and 32-yard touchdown passes to Andre Rison and Terance Mathis as the Falcons beat the Tampa Bay Buccaneers 34-13. The Atlanta fans were happy with their first-place team's 4-2 record. But they knew the Falcons had not beaten a quality team in 1994, so their enthusiasm was guarded. Besides, Atlanta had to play the 49ers and Deion Sanders the following week for sole possession of first place.

In the second quarter of that game. Sanders got into a fist fight with Rison. Later in the quarter, Sanders intercepted a Jeff George pass and ran 93 yards for a touchdown that helped the 49ers rout the stunned Falcons 42-3. Afterwards, Sanders apologized to Rison. But it was the Falcons who should have apologized to their fans.

In Week 8, Atlanta faced another quality team in the Los Angeles Raiders. Once again, the team came up empty, dropping the game 30-21. Atlanta was 4-4 and in second place. But they trailed the 49ers by two games.

After a bye, the Falcons faced one of the best teams in the NFL. The San Diego Chargers had a 7-1 record and one of the league's toughest defenses. So what did the Falcons do? They beat the Chargers in a defensive struggle, 10-9.

The following week, the Falcons played a team they could beat. But the New Orleans Saints matched the Falcons score for score and eked out a surprising 33-32 win. The loss evened Atlanta's record at 5-5 and put them three games behind the 49ers. First place seemed out of reach. But the playoffs still remained a good possibility.

But one week later, the playoff hopes began to tumble. Atlanta lost 32-28 to the Denver Broncos. After a 28-21 win over Philadelphia, the Falcons suffered another humiliating defeat to the 49ers, this time 50-14. Unable to rebound as they had all year, the Falcons lost again in Week 15, 29-20 to the Saints. Now their record was 6-8. They would have to win the rest of their games to ensure a playoff berth.

The Falcons Andre Rison (80) catches a touchdown pass against the Chargers at the Hall of Fame game, 1994.

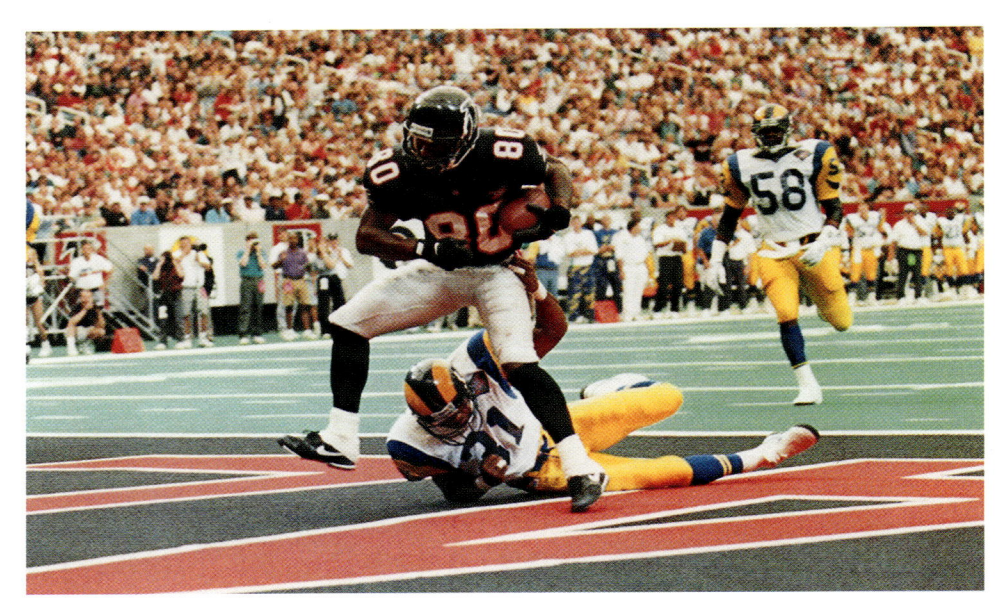

Andre Rison (80) catches a touchdown pass against the Los Angeles Rams.

However, a 21-17 loss to the Green Bay Packers put an end to Atlanta's thin playoff hopes. Atlanta had the game nearly won. But Green Bay's quarterback, Brett Favre, scrambled nine yards for the winning score with 14 seconds remaining and no time outs left. Atlanta rallied in the final week for a 10-6 win over the Arizona Cardinals. But their 7-9 record only earned them third place in the NFC West.

§

As they had been in the past, the Falcons remain a team in search of a star who can lead them to the playoffs. Jeff George still has the potential to be a great quarterback—not just a passer. But he needs to become a team leader. Without the likes of Deion Sanders, the Falcons cannot expect to soar to the top of the NFL.

GLOSSARY

ALL-PRO—A player who is voted to the Pro Bowl.

BACKFIELD—Players whose position is behind the line of scrimmage.

CORNERBACK—Either of two defensive halfbacks stationed a short distance behind the linebackers and relatively near the sidelines.

DEFENSIVE END—A defensive player who plays on the end of the line and often next to the defensive tackle.

DEFENSIVE TACKLE—A defensive player who plays on the line and between the guard and end.

ELIGIBLE—A player who is qualified to be voted into the Hall of Fame.

END ZONE—The area on either end of a football field where players score touchdowns.

EXTRA POINT—The additional one-point score added after a player makes a touchdown. Teams earn extra points if the placekicker kicks the ball through the uprights of the goalpost, or if an offensive player crosses the goal line with the football before being tackled.

FIELD GOAL—A three-point score awarded when a placekicker kicks the ball through the uprights of the goalpost.

FULLBACK—An offensive player who often lines up farthest behind the front line.

FUMBLE—When a player loses control of the football.

GUARD—An offensive lineman who plays between the tackles and center.

GROUND GAME—The running game.

HALFBACK—An offensive player whose position is behind the line of scrimmage.

HALFTIME—The time period between the second and third quarters of a football game.

INTERCEPTION—When a defensive player catches a pass from an offensive player.

KICK RETURNER—An offensive player who returns kickoffs.

LINEBACKER—A defensive player whose position is behind the line of scrimmage.

LINEMAN—An offensive or defensive player who plays on the line of scrimmage.

PASS—To throw the ball.

PASS RECEIVER—An offensive player who runs pass routes and catches passes.

PLACEKICKER—An offensive player who kicks extra points and field goals. The placekicker also kicks the ball from a tee to the opponent after his team has scored.

PLAYOFFS—The postseason games played amongst the division winners and wild card teams which determines the Super Bowl champion.
PRO BOWL—The postseason All-Star game which showcases the NFL's best players.
PUNT—To kick the ball to the opponent.
QUARTER—One of four 15-minute time periods that makes up a football game.
QUARTERBACK—The backfield player who usually calls the signals for the plays.
REGULAR SEASON—The games played after the preseason and before the playoffs.
ROOKIE—A first-year player.
RUNNING BACK—A backfield player who usually runs with the ball.
RUSH—To run with the football.
SACK—To tackle the quarterback behind the line of scrimmage.
SAFETY—A defensive back who plays behind the linemen and linebackers. Also, two points awarded for tackling an offensive player in his own end zone when he's carrying the ball.
SPECIAL TEAMS—Squads of football players that perform special tasks (for example, kickoff team and punt-return team).
SPONSOR—A person or company that finances a football team.
SUPER BOWL—The NFL Championship game played between the AFC champion and the NFC champion.
T FORMATION—An offensive formation in which the fullback lines up behind the center and quarterback with one halfback stationed on each side of the fullback.
TACKLE—An offensive or defensive lineman who plays between the ends and the guards.
TAILBACK—The offensive back farthest from the line of scrimmage.
TIGHT END—An offensive lineman who is stationed next to the tackles, and who usually blocks or catches passes.
TOUCHDOWN—When one team crosses the goal line of the other team's end zone. A touchdown is worth six points.
TURNOVER—To turn the ball over to an opponent either by a fumble, an interception, or on downs.
UNDERDOG—The team that is picked to lose the game.
WIDE RECEIVER—An offensive player who is stationed relatively close to the sidelines and who usually catches passes.
WILD CARD—A team that makes the playoffs without winning its division.
ZONE PASS DEFENSE—A pass defense method where defensive backs defend a certain area of the playing field rather than individual pass receivers.

INDEX

A

All-Pro 15
Andrews, William 12, 13, 15
Archer, David 15
Arizona Cardinals 28
Auburn University 12

B

Bartkowski, Steve 9, 11, 14, 15
baseball 21, 24
Bennett, Leeman 11, 12
Buffalo Bills 8, 12

C

Cain, Lynn 12
Campbell, Marion 16
Case, Scott 16
championships 14, 23
Clark, Vinnie 25
Coffey, Junior 6
Cribbs, Joe 12

D

Dallas Cowboys 6, 11, 14, 15
Denver Broncos 26
division title 4

F

Favre, Brett 28
Florida State University 20
Fralic, Bill 15, 23

G

George, Jeff 4, 25, 26, 28
Glanville, Jerry 22, 23, 24
Green Bay Packers 28

H

Hanifan, Jim 16
Hawkins, Alex 6
Haynes, Michael 23, 24
Hebert, Bobby 24
Hecker, Norb 8
Houston Oilers 6, 22
Humphrey, Claude 8

J

Johnson, Billy "White Shoes" 6, 15
Johnson, Norm 23, 24
Johnson, Randy 6
Jones, June 11, 24, 25

L

Lee, Bob 8
Los Angeles Raiders 26
Los Angeles Rams 22, 25

M

Mathis, Terance 25
McQuilken, Kim 8
Miller, Chris 16, 22-24
Minnesota Vikings 8
Montana, Joe 25
MVP 23

31

N

New Orleans 23, 26
New York Yankees 21, 22
NFC West 25, 28
NFL 8, 13, 23, 24, 25, 26, 28
Nobis, Tommy 6, 8

P

Pearson, Drew 15
Pegram, Erric 24
Philadelphia Eagles 11, 26
playoffs 4, 8, 9, 11, 14, 23, 24, 26, 28
Pritchard, Mike 24

R

Rassas, Nick 6
Reaves, Ken 6
Riggle, Bob 6
Riggs, Gerald 15
Rison 23, 24, 25, 26
Rookie of the Year 8

S

San Diego Chargers 26
San Francisco 49ers 24
Sanders, Deion 4, 16, 20, 21, 22, 23, 24, 26, 28
Seattle Mariners 22
Settle, John 16, 23
St. Louis Cardinals 8
Sullivan, Pat 8
Super Bowl 4, 9, 11, 14, 15

T

Tampa Bay Buccaneers 25
Tennessee State University 8

U

University of California 9
University of Texas 6

V

Van Brocklin, Norm 8

W

Washington Redskins 23, 25
White, Danny 11, 15
Wilson, Wade 24